Wright Middle

DIGITAL ENTREPRENEURSHIP™
IN THE AGE OF APPS, THE WEB, AND MOBILE DEVICES

GOING LIVE

LAUNCHING YOUR DIGITAL BUSINESS

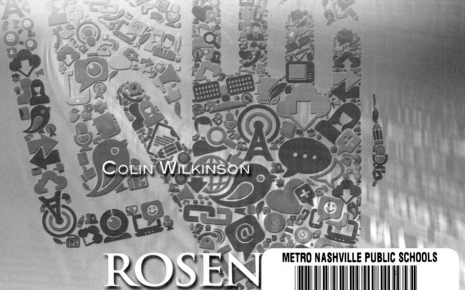

COLIN WILKINSON

ROSEN
PUBLISHING

New York

To Mom, for always encouraging my continued learning, and for remaining the most valued customer in everything I do.

Published in 2013 by The Rosen Publishing Group, Inc.
29 East 21st Street, New York, NY 10010

Library of Congress Cataloging-in-Publication Data

Wilkinson, Colin, 1977–
Going live: launching your digital business/Colin Wilkinson.
—1st ed.
    p. cm.—(Digital entrepreneurship in the age of apps, the Web, and mobile devices)
Includes bibliographical references and index.
ISBN 978-1-4488-6927-5 (library binding: alk. paper)—
ISBN 978-1-4488-6972-5 (pbk.: alk. paper)—
ISBN 978-1-4488-6973-2 (6-pack: alk. paper)
1. Internet software industry. 2. Application software—Development. 3. New products—Management. 4. New business enterprises—Management. I. Title.
HD9696.65.A2W55 2013
005.068'1—dc23
                                                                    2012004245

Manufactured in the United States of America

CPSIA Compliance Information: Batch #S12YA: For further information, contact Rosen Publishing, New York, New York, at 1-800-237-9932.

CONTENTS

INTROD

S tarting any business is full of risks and rewards, but with a digital business, you can often reduce your risk with proper planning. The ability to make live updates—adding content or fixing problems after the product has launched—opens up an entirely new realm of possibilities and responsibility. Building a successful product for online consumption requires a working knowledge of the technology being used and a familiarity with the audience and the competition. With new tools appearing regularly, making the job of constructing Web sites and apps easier, it's possible to dive in with little or even no prior experience and come out with a hit product.

Becoming a digital entrepreneur can be a daunting task. The steps needed to transform a great idea into a successful product can be many. Even the process of

finding the right audience and platform (such as Facebook, iPhone, Android, or a Web site) can be a difficult choice to make. What's more, these technologies are changing constantly, growing with new hardware and expanding into new markets. By studying the process of design and development—and the importance of continued product support—today's developer can make informed decisions. The developer can also balance risks versus rewards in order to target a trouble-free launch. This book looks at the creative process leading to a successful digital product launch.

Digital entrepreneur Albert Ko maintains his bargain-hunting Web site CheapCheapCheap.com from his home office.

CHAPTER 1

DESIGNING YOUR DIGITAL PRODUCT

The first step in developing a great idea into a successful product and business is to work out the details. In the design phase, you must answer important questions about the look and feel of the product, the goals and priorities for its creation, and the factors most likely to lead to a hit. For example, how does the user interact with the app, play the game, or navigate the Web site? Focusing on the key features—the memorable aspects that separate this product from others currently available—is a great way to get started.

RESEARCHING THE COMPETITION

An important factor in any good business plan is a thorough understanding of the market. For app developers, this may mean researching what is available in the app stores, what users are saying in their reviews, and what their prices are. For blogs or other Web-based products, taking a look at popular sites and the level of user engagement may be the way to go.

Taking time to use competitive products can be a great way to get new ideas and solve problems while developing your own product. Keeping an organized set of notes on reference apps, games, and Web sites iPad 🔋   10:34 AM   100% 🔋

Top Charts

Categories

TOP PAID iPad APPS

1. Penultimate
Productivity
Released Apr 16, 2010
★★★★½ 574 Ratings
$0.99

2. Angry Birds HD
Games
Released Apr 01, 2010
★★★★★ 6488 Ratings
$4.99

3. World of Goo
Games
Released Dec 16, 2010
★★★★½ 1019 Ratings
$4.99

4. Pages
Productivity
Released Apr 01, 2010
★★★★☆ 585 Ratings
$9.99

5. Cut the Rope HD
Games
Released Oct 07, 2010
★★★★★ 1701 Ratings
$1.99

6. Fruit Ninja HD
Games
Released Jul 14, 2010
★★★★½ 5401 Ratings
$2.99

7. Facepad+ - Facebook for ...
Social Networking
Released Jan 11, 2011
★★½☆☆ 41 Ratings
$0.99

8. Angry Birds Seasons HD
Games
Released Oct 21, 2010
★★★★½ 3618 Ratings
$1.99

TOP FREE iPad APPS

1. Angry Birds HD Free
Games
Released Jan 05, 2011
★★★★½ 2951 Ratings
FREE

2. Mr Giggle HD Lite
Games
Released Jan 06, 2011
★★★★★ 1851 Ratings
FREE

3. Deer Hunter Challenge
Games
Released Dec 01, 2010
★★★★☆ 18296 Ratings
FREE

4. Virtuoso Piano Free 3
Music
Released Jan 05, 2011
★★★★☆ 122 Ratings
FREE

5. Angry Birds Seasons HD ...
Games
Released Jan 05, 2011
★★★★☆ 949 Ratings
FREE

6. Facepad - Facebook for i...
Social Networking
Released Dec 29, 2010
★★★☆☆ 309 Ratings
FREE

7. RobotNGunHD
Games
Released Dec 11, 2010
★★★★☆ 19 Ratings
FREE

8. The Treasures of Mystery...
Games
Released Jan 13, 2011
★★★★☆ 57 Ratings
FREE

Genius   Top Charts   Categories   Updates

Keeping an eye on the top downloads and what their users are saying on platforms like Apple's App Store is a great way to learn about successful product design.

can prove invaluable while developing and updating your digital product.

When doing this research, it's important to review failures as well as successes. Understanding how to fail, and how to avoid failure, is a vital part of finding success. Thomas Edison once said, "I have not failed. I've just found ten thousand ways that won't work." An entrepreneur can avoid some pitfalls by observing what works—and what doesn't—in similar products already available. Notice what features users request in their reviews and how they are addressed, if at all. Observe the frequency and extent of product updates, rankings on popular search engines, and how businesses communicate with their customers. Observations like these can be the best way to build off of the experience of others.

THE LIVING DESIGN

A design document communicates your vision for a digital product, and your plan for developing it, in enough detail to implement it. It's a dynamic, living document: it's expected to change over time and often has multiple authors. This allows details to be filled in when necessary and adjusted when the design changes. Documentation can improve communication among a team, even when people are working remotely. It's a good idea to save occasional backups of the design, both to refer back to as a history of the design and as an opportunity to undo any missteps.

When designing, keep in mind that images can often be more effective at communicating than text.

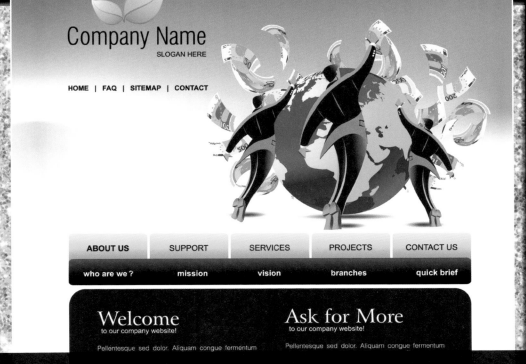

Great product design is not just about content. Working with prototypes allows details such as the layout, color scheme, and navigation to be defined up front.

You can use flowcharts to demonstrate the menus of an app and how they connect to one another, character illustrations for a video game, or even a simple sketch to represent the layout of a Web site. You'd be surprised at how many successful apps started out as a sketch on a napkin.

Planning visually can be especially useful when developing a user interface, one of the most important aspects of any digital product. The user interface is the place where the user interacts with the game, app, or Web site. Designing it includes general items such as fonts, colors, and screen layout. It also includes the design of widgets—elements that the user can alter such as buttons, drop-down menus, and scrolling lists. A visual design can help generate team conversation and stimulate additional planning. This can drastically reduce the overall amount of time for finishing the product, since there will be fewer unknowns when implementing it.

While it's possible to have a single-person development force, learning to work with a team can lead to a more well-rounded and successful digital product. However, designing with a team can present its own challenges. To help with the process of group design, tools for team documentation, such as wiki pages, shared document services, and cloud computer storage, can prove very useful. Carefully documenting and reviewing the design with the team will help ensure that everyone is on the same page.

PLANNING FOR SUCCESS

When designing your product, it's essential to determine who the end user is. Knowing what sort of person you're targeting can have a big impact on your product's design. It's worth thinking about the audience's age, typical environment and behavior, and products they use. Creating a successful product means catering to the needs of this audience. Work with the audience as much as possible every step of the way, from design to launch to later updates.

YOUNG DIGITAL ENTREPRENEURS

Many of today's successful digital entrepreneurs started their businesses in their teens or early twenties. The following are some notable young digital entrepreneurs:

- Matt Mullenweg started the popular blogging service WordPress when he was eighteen.
- Siblings Catherine and David Cook started MyYearBook.com in 2005 when they were teenagers.
- Aaron Levie and Dylan Smith started the file sharing and cloud storage service Box.net before graduating from college.
- Ashley Qualls started her multimillion-dollar ad-supported venture WhatEverLife.com with just $8 at age fourteen.
- Mark Zuckerberg, who founded Facebook while he was in college, is the world's youngest billionaire.

Testing early versions of the product with its typical user can be a boon to the development process. Gaining firsthand experience with the choices that users make and how they respond to various interface

Matt Mullenweg, developer and founder of WordPress, began his work on the popular blogging software when he was eighteen. Millions of Web sites now run on it.

designs will help shape a successful product. It can also give you information for other parts of your business, like advertising and product support. This practice of designing a product with the end user in mind above all else is known as user-centered design.

It can be helpful to have a clear definition of what success means for your product during the design phase. Profitability, measured in earnings, is not always going to be the ideal measurement for success, especially in the beginning. For instance, perhaps your goal is to maximize downloads of your app so that, down the road, an advertising component can be integrated. A Web site or blog may be looking to reach a certain number of regular readers posting comments and sharing stories across the Web. Keep these goals in mind so that you and your team can develop a product you can be proud of.

Finally, special attention must be paid to a plan for future updates. Today's digital products allow for updates, patches, fixes, and additions in response to error reports, user feedback, and praise. These updates are no longer just a possibility; users of today's apps, Web sites, and games expect them.

When planning for future updates, think about what features might be expanded upon. For instance, you might add more levels to a game or new ways to connect with other users of a blog. Successful digital entrepreneurs also use metrics to improve their product's performance. This is information gathered about the users and how they use the product. Collecting data can be as simple as providing users with a method for reviewing the product or as detailed as storing a record of the errors users have encountered. Other useful information can include the times of day when users are accessing the product, how they found it, and what features they use the most.

What specific data can be gathered and what will be most useful depends on the product being developed, but it's worth considering throughout the design phase. Research can come in handy to see how similar products gather and utilize metrics.

CHAPTER 2

SELECTING YOUR WORKFLOW

The process used to create a digital product can directly influence the quality of the final product. Selecting the proper tools, workflow, and methods of communication among your team will help minimize frustration and confusion throughout the development process. Understanding the options available and choosing carefully before diving into production can boost productivity and contribute to the team's experience.

SELECTING SOFTWARE AND HARDWARE

An important step during the design phase is considering what is required to develop your product. Some products may have obvious choices. For instance, iPhone and iPad development must be done on an Apple computer with an Intel processor because this is the only combination that will run the development software. Other types of products have a broader set of requirements. For instance, creating a Web site can be done in nearly any piece of software that allows one to edit text. It can also be done entirely online through a Web browser using an online Web site editor.

Also consider what software you will need to create any graphics used in the product. While there are very

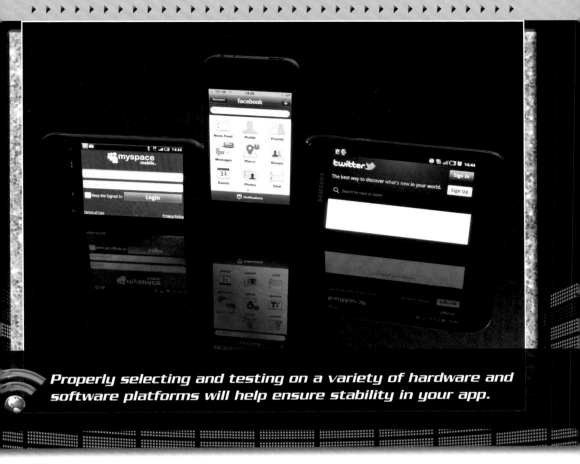

Properly selecting and testing on a variety of hardware and software platforms will help ensure stability in your app.

powerful software suites for this kind of work, it may be worthwhile to investigate less expensive, or even free, alternatives. If you are working with a team, it's likely that all team members will need access to these tools. It's often best to start with what is freely available and then branch out after finding some success.

Decide what technology you are targeting with your product. When building an app, you'll need to identify which devices to support, as they often have varied screen sizes and graphics capabilities. For Web

Wright Middle

sites and blogs, you'll need to discuss which browsers and versions to support, as well as what size monitors the Web site should display on without the need for scrolling to reach content.

In making these decisions, it's important to consider the end user. Often, this means developing for the widest range of users. For instance, when developing a game for Apple iOS, it can be a quick decision to target the latest and greatest iPhone as a platform. However, in doing this, you may be overlooking the successful iPod Touch device, which is more frequently used by younger gamers. With Android devices, a wide variety of capabilities, operating systems, and screen resolutions are on the market, so pinpointing which devices will run the app is a decision to make early on.

In addition to software, consider any hardware needs. It's unlikely that someone will own all the smartphones or tablets they are developing for, or that they'll have immediate access to a broad set of computers with a variety of graphical, processor, or Internet bandwidth constraints. The best methods for developing digital apps, games, and Web sites call for testing on all target platforms to ensure stability and a quality user experience. When that's not possible, some shortcuts may be needed.

During the design process, identify the minimum system requirements for your product: the slowest, oldest, or least powerful device the product will safely run on. Once this has been determined, it can be a good benchmark for testing and development. Test on the

WORKING AS A TEAM

Each member of a development team plays a key role in the creation and maintenance of the product. Common team roles for digital product development include:

- **Producer or project manager.** Managers oversee production schedules and facilitate team communication. They may also be in charge of client relations.
- **Designer.** Designers provide the vision for a product. They may specialize in certain areas, such as audio design or user interface design.
- **Programmer.** Programmers write the code that drives the product. Some may focus on specific areas, such as network or database needs.
- **Artist.** Artists provide the visuals and direction for the look and feel of the product, as well as colors, fonts, and other graphics that brand the product.

Support roles may include testers or people with specialized areas of expertise, such as handling the submission process for a mobile app.

widest variety of possible user setups. When the minimum system isn't available, there are tools that will allow you to do the job. Setting a computer's screen resolution to something smaller, to mimic a smaller monitor, can be incredibly useful when developing Web site layouts. Emulators, software that imitates other devices, can be used in the absence of mobile phone and other types of hardware. Be aware that testing on an emulator is never going to fully replace testing on the actual hardware.

Software engineers and a designer discuss a Web display for the clothing company Bonobos. Working as a team allows expertise from various disciplines to shape a high-quality digital product.

SHARED STORAGE

An essential aspect of the development workflow is deciding where to store the work. On a team venture, there are immediate benefits to finding a storage solution that allows all team members to access the work being done. Even when working solo, using a storage solution protects the work from hard drive failures and other digital disasters. There are several types of storage you can use.

The simplest involves storing the project work in one central location that can be accessed by all team members. This might be an external hard drive or USB memory stick. Or it could be an online location, such as an FTP server, that allows files to be uploaded and downloaded. In this approach, members copy or download files from the central storage to their computers to do their work. When finished, they upload the new and changed files back to the storage device. The primary drawback is that developers must always make sure the latest files are downloaded before working. This approach also makes it difficult for more than one person to work on a given file at one time. Any changes made in parallel need to be merged, which can be a very error-prone process. As a result, this type of central storage is often most useful for creating backups, or snapshots, of the project as it develops.

An alternative that has been gaining popularity—to the point that it has become a built-in feature for many smartphones—is cloud storage. What makes cloud storage so useful is that, rather than storing files directly on one's computer, files are uploaded to an online storage service known as the cloud. Files on the cloud can be downloaded to multiple locations and various devices, and they can be shared with others. Best of all, the uploading and downloading are handled entirely by the software to help eliminate user error. When working with cloud storage, the user identifies a folder on the computer to be stored to the cloud. Each time files are opened or edited from within this folder, the current version is downloaded from the cloud; when the file is saved and closed, it is uploaded back to the cloud. This helps ensure that the work being done is always current.

While cloud storage solves many team woes, it can still create difficulties when multiple developers edit the same files simultaneously. To solve this problem, many experienced teams have turned to version control software. With version control, each change made to any file is saved separately, creating a history for the project. As team members work together, even in the same files, the changes made by each one are stored individually and then merged into a final document. Developers can correct errors they discover by stepping back into the file's history and selectively removing changes made along the way. Setting up a version control system can be a chore. Luckily, some ready-made online services are available for smaller teams in need of a versioning solution.

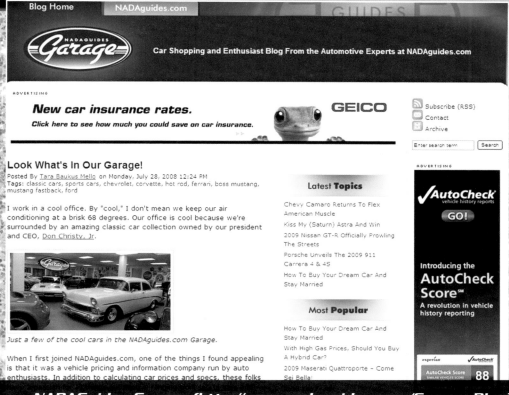

NADAGuides Garage (http://www.nadaguides.com/Garage-Blog) is a blog for car enthusiasts. A blog concept that attracts regular user traffic can be a good match for focused advertising.

PLANNING FOR PROFIT

When developing a digital product, consider the potential profitability of your product and your means to reaching this profit.

When planning for monetization—collecting money from your product's customers—there are many paths to take. Products may be sold to the user for a price,

A PayPal representative demonstrates how the application works on an iPad at a company event. Many digital entrepreneurs use prepackaged solutions such as PayPal for collecting donations and payments.

or they may be free for the user with financial support from ads or in-app purchases. Web sites and blogs often find their profits in advertising, sometimes teaming up with specific partners who share an audience with them. Other sites earn money through paid memberships granting additional access and benefits.

When trying to judge the potential profitability of your product, the most effective approach is to look at reference products already on the market. Consider their costs to the user, how they present any advertising, and how often the user is prompted to make any sort of purchase.

Also consider your audience: Are they likely to spend $5 to download your app, or is $1 a more reasonable target?

Recent trends have shown the strength of planning for in-app purchases. According to an article on GigaOM.com, many top-grossing iPhone apps are free initially but make their money from in-app purchases. Examples of in-app purchases are bonus levels, maps, virtual currency, or points to advance your character in a game. Outside of gaming, in-app purchases may include subscriptions for ongoing access, recurring services, or premium services.

When predicting profits, consider costs you'll incur along the way. For instance, online app stores often take a percentage of each sale. Even payment processing systems apply a fee to each transaction. While these are often small, they can add up quickly. Incorporating these expenses into your plan will help you avoid being caught off guard as the profits begin flowing in.

With mobile apps, developers are typically required to use built-in solutions for collecting payments. With Web products, however, the development team is often responsible for setting up the payment processing themselves. There are many possible solutions for accepting payments. The most popular are PayPal, Amazon Payments, and Google Checkout. When review-ing payment solutions, the key factors to consider are the fees to your business per transaction; the ease with which the payments can be integrated into the product; and the availability of any online tools for tracking and managing payments and studying sales metrics.

CHAPTER 3

ENTERING PRODUCTION

Shifting from design and planning to production of your product, including creating the art and code, is a major step. When this transition goes smoothly, it can lead to a higher-quality product and a positive process for the team. Understanding the steps needed to create the product, as well as the tools and techniques used during production, will help you commit to a final design and move forward with confidence.

CHOOSING A DEVELOPMENT PROCESS

There are many approaches you can use to structure the development of your product. An organized approach can help the development team become better performers and a more tightly knit group. Understanding the strengths of each approach, as well as its pitfalls, can help you choose a process that fits the project's need and the team's workflow.

The most frequently used process is the waterfall model, so called because of its linear nature. In this process, each phase of production lives independently of the other. Any given phase comes to completion before the next phase is begun. The waterfall process works well for short projects and can be straightforward to use. However, it adds risk because there is little to

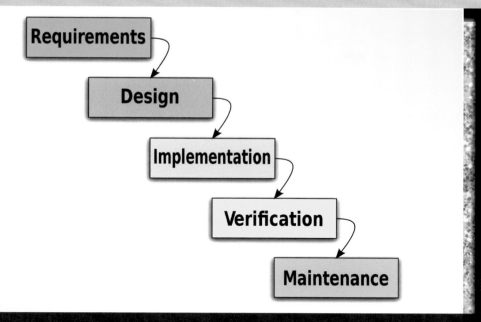

Development processes, such as the waterfall model shown here, add structure and organization to the creative approach used when building successful products.

no working product until late into development. Also, it may make ongoing projects, including those supported by updates, cumbersome.

Another popular development processes is the iterative process, sometimes referred to as an "agile" process. The iterative process is similar in flow to the waterfall process but is divided into smaller chunks of production with a full cycle of planning, design, implementation, and testing during each step. Development is faster, yielding working code earlier. This allows for changes to design and scope with minimal added risk (hence, its "agile" moniker). The downside of the rapid nature of iterative development is that you may not have time for full planning and research of many of the design details, creating bugs and logistics issues with the software down the road.

Additional processes, including the spiral and prototype methods, seek to solve some drawbacks of the iterative and waterfall methodologies, but make trade-offs by adding time, risk, or complexity. In the end, the process used by any given team should be adjusted to fit the team's needs. If the process is getting in the way of creative development, it's not doing its job.

DEVELOPING A MOBILE APP

Developing a mobile app can be a rewarding experience. Mobile phone makers have put a lot of thought and money into making the job of a developer as easy as possible.

To develop for mobile phones and other mobile devices, one must first register as a developer. Registration includes consenting to a licensing agreement and, in some cases, a onetime fee. Once this is done, the developer gains access to the development Web site, documentation, samples, and, most important, the software development kit (SDK) used to create apps for the mobile platform. The SDK is where the bulk of the work is done, using project templates to get things moving quickly.

To get started, create a new project and give it a name. This will automatically put some code in place

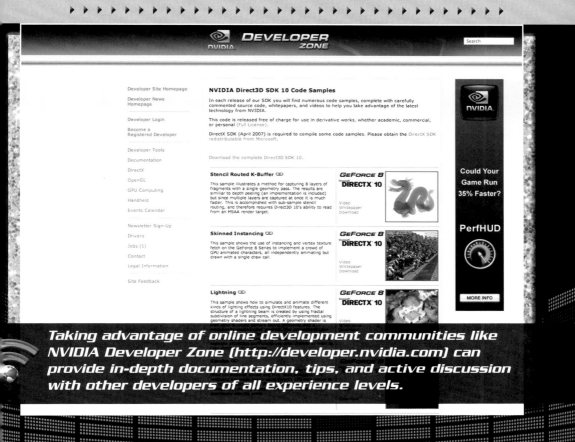

Taking advantage of online development communities like NVIDIA Developer Zone (http://developer.nvidia.com) can provide in-depth documentation, tips, and active discussion with other developers of all experience levels.

that will help get the application up and running quickly. You won't ever have to worry about these items, making more time for the fun side of development. Now that a new project has been opened, there are a lot of directions you can go in. Usually, the first step is to create a "hello world" application, a simple application that prints the text "hello world" to the device's screen. iOS software is typically created using the Objective-C programming language, while Android apps are created using Java. Both platforms are making allowances for other programming languages as well.

For a basic comparison, here is what a typical "hello world" program might look like in these two languages:

Objective-C:
```
#include <stdio.h>
int main(void)
{
 printf("Hello, World!");
 return;
}
```

Java:
```
public class HelloWorld {
 public static void main(String[] args) {
  System.out.println("Hello, World");
 }
}
```

Each SDK includes tutorials for creating a basic "hello world" application; these should be among the first destinations for a new developer. The tutorials take the user through the steps of building an application and running it within the simulator, a software stand-in that mimics an iPhone or Android device directly on the development computer. While there is a lot more that goes into a typical application, the "hello world" application, in essence, contains all the important structure and action needed to lay the groundwork for any type of application. In fact, by building off of this application and adding new elements and functions—pieces of code that can have an input and output, or which may be manipulated in some way—a beginning developer can work toward building the app of his or her own design.

Mobile application SDKs have many tools that make creating applications easier. For instance, the Apple SDK includes a powerful piece of software called Interface Builder, which can be used to quickly create powerful, complex user interfaces. It can be used to generate code that responds to interface elements. Both SDKs include tools for optimizing the code by tracking memory and resource usage, allowing developers to identify potential problems in the software. The SDK toolset even includes built-in solutions to aid in the process of preparing and publishing the final product to the online store.

DEVELOPING WEB SITES AND BLOGS

Creating Web sites is a great way to enter the world of digital entrepreneurship, as there is very little cost to get started and the bulk of the work can be done in any text editor. A Web server is needed to share the site with others online. There are many options with a wide range of price tags.

The simplest form of Web site coding is done in HTML, or HyperText Markup Language, which is made up of a series of tags and keywords contained within angle brackets that define HTML elements. Usually, each tag has a closing tag, denoted by a forward slash.

The most basic Web page only requires a set of tags defining the type of page:

```
<html>
</html>
```

Typing these two simple lines into a text editor and saving the file with the ".html" extension creates the most basic Web page. In fact, that file could be safely loaded into a Web browser to generate HTML output, even if it may be a bit boring. A more polished example illustrates the two main components of a Web page: the head, which specifies properties not displayed on the page, and the body, which contains content displayed in the Web browser's window:

```
<html>
<head>
<title>Hello World!</title>
</head>

<body>
Hello World!
</body>
</html>
```

Most other elements—including images, links, lists, and interactive forms—follow the same format. With some research and practice, a Web developer can build great-looking sites in no time. Making this even simpler,

READY-MADE DEVELOPMENT SOLUTIONS FOR WEB SITES, BLOGS, AND GAMES

These popular ready-made development solutions can help you reach your goals for your digital business more easily:

- WordPress is a free blogging solution complete with customizable themes and layouts.

- Text editors with built-in formatting, including Notepad++, make a great environment for writing code and building Web sites.

- Visual Web site editors, including Dreamweaver and CoffeeCup, allow people to build great-looking sites without having to dive into the code.

- GameMaker allows developers to quickly build rich and engaging games and share them online, using a unique visual editing interface.

many Web hosts have site-building software that can speed up the process. There are also free blog-hosting software packages that handle most of the work, allowing a developer to focus on writing a fantastic blog.

Many extensions and alternatives to basic HTML have emerged, each offering something unique. More control over the look and feel of a Web page can be created using

Cascading Style Sheets, or CSS. CSS language allows developers to define a set of visual styles (fonts, colors, borders, etc.) that can be inherited across multiple pages. Data lists can be generated and referenced, similar to using a spreadsheet, with the use of XML (Extensible Markup Language) or databases. In fact, databases can be used to gather and store data from users, such as information from a feedback form. Other technologies, including various forms of scripts, cater to interactivity and a dynamic site presentation, either on the user's computer with scripting languages like JavaScript or on the server itself using languages including PHP or ASP.

A helpful feature for developers is that, typically, all the content from a Web page is downloaded to the user's computer. This means that the source code for the page itself, and any scripts embedded within the page, can be viewed directly and used for reference. With practice, reading a Web page's source file can become straightforward, allowing a developer to see how some-one else may have implemented a snazzy drop-down menu or a dynamic layout. By investigating what other developers are doing, and building on that with the tools and technologies available, a digital entrepreneur can continually work with fantastic new styles of Web devel-opment and create exciting new Web site designs.

GETTING STARTED WITH MONETIZATION

Monetization is important for any successful digital busi-ness. One popular approach is to support your product with advertising. Ads can work well for all types of digital products, and advertising solutions make it simple to include them on a Web site or app. Tools like Google AdSense do all the legwork for generating ads, requiring only some initial setup followed by a quick copy-and-paste of relevant HTML code. Mobile app developers also have straightforward solutions for gaining revenue from advertising, with programs like Apple's iAd.

A more direct method of monetizing is to sell additional content or services using online payment systems. For collecting payments online, PayPal provides a no-nonsense setup with tools for generating donation buttons, payment forms, and even full-fledged shopping cart systems with simple copy-and-paste generated code. Once a PayPal account has been created, it can be linked to a bank account to easily deposit earnings. Other Web solutions include proprietary currencies for handling purchases, such as Facebook's Credits. These include their own documentation and specialized code for handling the transactions and can be a great alternative to accepting credit cards directly.

In-app purchases are another option for monetization. They can be very rewarding when used properly. In-app purchases may include subscriptions, onetime purchases, or "consumable" items that are popular in mobile games. Consumable items are essentially used up immediately upon purchase and must be repurchased each time the user needs them.

To add in-app purchases to an iOS application, the developer adds the purchasable content using the

Dove's Men+Care product line was the first to take advantage of Apple's iAd advertising on the iPad with touch-driven interactive elements.

developer administration Web site and then writes the code to make the purchasable content available. This process can vary from one app to the next. Any developer's first step should be to review the sample code for in-app purchases (in-app billing on the Android) that is bundled with the SDK.

CHAPTER 4

IMPROVING THE PRODUCT THROUGH ITERATIVE DESIGN

Iterative design is a process of design and development that allows for frequent review and adjustment. It works well with the idea of a living design document, which is revised as the development team refines their approach. Iteration may include art and interface mock-ups, gameplay or usability prototypes for testing, and even public releases of the prelaunch software for real user testing and feedback. Incorporating time into the schedule for iteration can help the product evolve more naturally into a success.

DEVELOPMENT MILESTONES

One downside of iterative design is that you can over-think a feature, iterating to the point that momentum on the project is lost. To help combat this concern, development milestones—development goals and dates for reaching them—are created.

The definition, number, and frequency of these milestones vary from project to project but typically involve an alpha milestone and beta milestone. An alpha milestone is the point at which all functionality is completed but the product may be lacking in polish and art. A beta milestone is the point at which the product is complete, minus small fixes. These milestones can be used as a point of reflection and review, and they help build momentum and a sense of accomplishment.

Determining a schedule for larger milestones up front, as well as definitions that can be agreed upon by the team, will help the product become a success. This schedule can also help separate core product features (needs) from wish list items that are out of scope for the project's time frame (wants). It's important to document any ideas that are cut from a project due to timing concerns. Don't just throw them out: these ideas could be the successful beginnings of a future update or another product entirely.

PROTOTYPE TESTING

Prototyping is a key aspect of iterative design. It allows new ideas to be designed, built, and tested quickly, without the added expense of detailed art and programming. At its core, a prototype is a test of ideas (or sometimes just one idea) that can be retested, reviewed, and adjusted. For instance, a prototype might include a simple menu layout, without actual interactive elements, that is put in front of users to see how they react and what elements they notice first. As prototypes are tested and updated based on findings, the team develops a concrete set of design principles that can be used to help shape the core interactions, look and feel, and overall appeal of the final product.

To get the most valuable feedback, find testers that could be considered members of your target audience. Also, due to the limited scope of each prototype,

A Study of Iterative Design: Netflix.com

The design team behind Netflix.com has to cater to an extremely wide audience, basically anyone who enjoys movies. The key to success has been iteration. If something doesn't work, they're not afraid to throw it out and try something else. The Netflix team has used a "try and see" approach in which they introduce new features to the site and then trim what doesn't stick during the next iteration. In fact, this iterative process of designing new features, implementing them, and watching the users' reaction before tweaking, improving, or even cutting the changes happens every two weeks at Netflix.com.

test with a focus in mind. Have a set of questions the prototype is intended to answer. A gameplay prototype intended to test how fun it feels for the game's character to run and jump may not provide any useful information on how rewarding the menu interactions are. When testing prototypes, it can be helpful to allow testers to talk through their experience and follow up with directed questions afterward. What did they like? What would they want to do differently? Watch for any difficulties the user seems to be having and work with your team to address them.

A tester works on a Halo game at Bungie headquarters in Washington State. Proper testing involves regimented documentation and repetitive tasks but yields a superior end user experience.

QUALITY ASSURANCE TESTING

Quality assurance testing, or QA testing, is used to identify functional problems with the product. These might include situations in which a button does not click, text is displaying incorrectly, or an application crashes unexpectedly. Quality testing is essential to delivering a successful product that users will want to revisit. It can even be required when releasing your product through certain digital distribution channels.

Quality testing typically begins in the latter half of the development schedule, and it often starts with a testing plan. The plan should list each part of the product, how it can be reached, and what the user can do from there. Think of it as a checklist of every possible thing the user can do. As the tester works down the list, any errors found should be recorded for the development team to investigate. Frequent testing will help ensure that the product is fully enjoyable at launch.

THE SOFT LAUNCH

Today's digital world makes it easy to update apps and make quick adjustments to Web sites in response to user feedback and metrics. Many products are taking

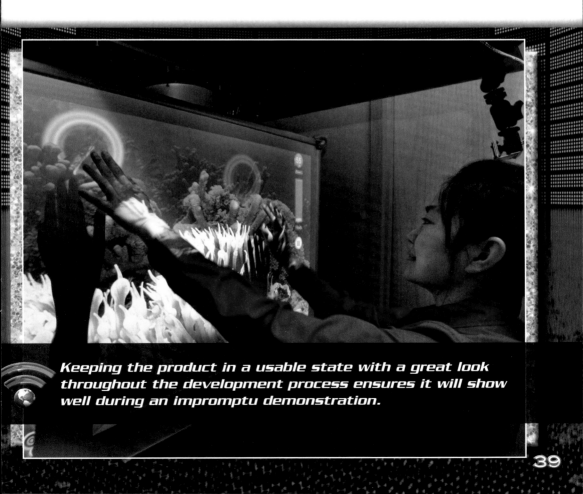

Keeping the product in a usable state with a great look throughout the development process ensures it will show well during an impromptu demonstration.

advantage of this with a soft launch. This is the process of releasing a product to a limited number of users, or with a limited number of features, with the plan to add more later on. When Google's popular Gmail service was first launched, it had only the most core features; the added functionality came later. Many Facebook apps and updates are initially launched to a small set of users so that the developers can identify problems, make adjustments for gameplay balancing, and find holes in the design before releasing them to the entire social network. When using a soft launch, it is important to identify what questions need to be answered and what information needs to be gathered to answer them.

PRE-SELLING

Pre-selling is the act of preparing or conditioning the user toward making a purchase. It can be done through advertising, making announcements about the product, or creating preview videos and posting them online. Advertising in venues that reach the target audience is important to the success of this strategy.

The more subtle aspects of pre-selling aim to give the users a sense of comfort and trust in the developer and the product. Besides building interest in the product and the features it provides, pre-selling can involve communication with users via regular updates and responding to reviews. It can work similarly to a soft launch, allowing the developer to gauge interest and collect feedback, even before the product is released.

CHAPTER 5

PRODUCT LAUNCH

When it's time for the big launch, nothing is more desirable than a trouble-free process. However, issues often arise that may not have been noticed during development. Knowing what to expect from the launch process—and being prepared for quick fixes as needed—requires careful planning. Before submitting an app, launching a Web site, or publishing a blog, have a plan in place for answering support e-mails, watching reviews and user comments, and responding to the approval process.

SUBMITTING AN APP

Launching a mobile app can be a bit tricky. There are many requirements for a successful launch into the App Store or Android Market. To start, both services require that the app be "signed" using a process that digitally ensures the app is what it claims to be, often embedding information about the author securely within. This avoids fraudulent updates and allows the original authors of an app to prove their ownership. These signatures are often used when releasing updates so that the store can tie the update to the correct app.

Each app must meet the requirements of the particular store it will be featured in. For instance, both major mobile app stores include specific formats for their content's naming, versioning, and icons. These are defined within their developer documentation. The app's size should be considered also. iOS devices only allow apps up to 20MB to be downloaded without a WiFi connection. The Android Market goes one step further and places a limit on the maximum file size for any application uploaded to the store.

There is a streamlined interface for uploading an app once the developer has tested and validated it. Depending on the app and the target market, more information, including screenshots and ratings information, may be

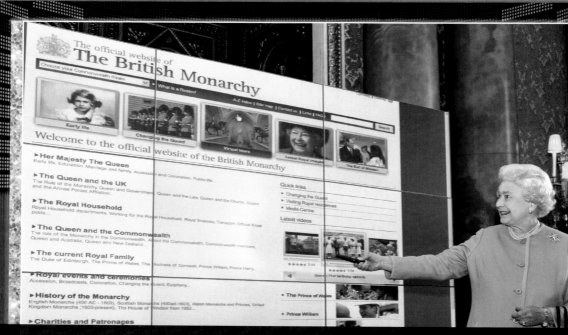

Launching a product, such as the updated British Monarchy Web site, is a time to celebrate all the hard work that went into its design and creation. Above, Queen Elizabeth II admires the site's new layout.

required. Be aware that submitting an app to be published does not always make it available right away.
For instance, Apple reviews all submitted apps, both
for content and stability, before they become available
for purchase and download. This process can take up
to two weeks and is used to keep objectionable applications from appearing in the App Store. Apple's
guidelines for this process are not public and can
change at any time. So remember the golden rule:
"If there is a doubt, it's best not to submit."

LAUNCHING A WEB SITE OR BLOG

The process of launching a Web site or blog requires the
same attention to detail as publishing a mobile app.
However, there is typically no formal process or reviewing agency involved. This pushes these important tasks
onto the developer. The downside is that content on the
Web is usually public and can be found by browsers and
search engines before it's meant to be seen. You can
address this problem by using a staging server or site,
sometimes in conjunction with a landing page.

The staging server acts as a sort of testing ground,
where the Web content can be viewed, tested, and
updated out of the public eye. The staging server doesn't
necessarily require a separate server; the test site can live
within a folder on the live site. By password protecting the
folder, which you can usually do through the Web host's
online tools, your site can be kept from prying eyes.
Once the site is ready to go live, the files can simply
be copied or uploaded into the main site directory.

The landing page is a default page that appears when users visit the Web site. It's called the landing page because it's the first page users see—it's where they land when visiting the site or blog. It can be used to announce a Web site that is "Coming Soon" or a blog that is "Undergoing Updates." Be sure not to leave a temporary landing page up for too long, as it can turn away users and create an incorrect impression of the site on search engines. By replacing this default page (typically, the "default," "home," or "index" file) last, the Web site is certain to be fully available by the time a user visits.

THE CUSTOMER IS ALWAYS RIGHT

The other half of launch preparation focuses less on the technical aspects of the product and more on other business concerns.

Choosing the timing for the launch can be key to its success. Once the time frame has been determined, consider the advertising efforts that will lead up to the launch. In some venues, such as the Apple App Store, the first twenty-four hours after the launch can be the most important. Announce the launch to users and followers via Facebook, Twitter, supporting Web sites, e-mail newsletter lists—whatever is available. Providing access to the site or app, early if possible, to key reviewers (who will hopefully share their enthusiasm with their readers) can be instrumental in creating a big launch, too.

The launch of the product—after much design, implementation, redesign, and bug fixing—is a time to celebrate. It's also a time to switch gears to supporting your product's user base. The more people who use your app, visit your Web site, or read your blog, the more opinions there will be on how to improve it. Keeping an eye on user reviews and feedback can be the best way to identify problems in the product, as well as any desired features for an upcoming release.

For a product to be successful long-term, the process of reviewing and responding to user input must be ongoing. Informing customers of what great features

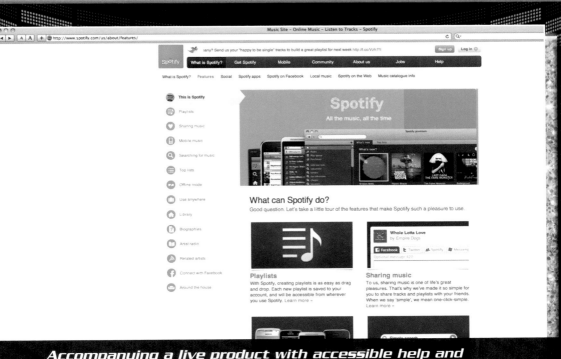

Accompanying a live product with accessible help and instruction encourages a positive user experience. This often results in favorable reviews and a more dedicated user base, as seen on sites like Spotify (http://www.spotify.com).

ON

and updates they can expect through a company's Web site, blog, or social media can be a great way to keep them coming back for more. A successful example is Bolt Creative's Pocket God app. What started as a simple iOS game has grown to reach users in various media, with regular updates publicized in a central blog. The blog incorporates fan-created art and contests to continually engage its audience.

ONGOING TESTING WITH STYLE

Not only do you need to support the product's users with frequent updates and communication, but you also need to support the product itself with ongoing testing for new features and updates. Thankfully, there are lots of ways to reduce the amount of effort required.

The simplest way to reduce time devoted to testing is to keep things organized. This can be as simple as maintaining a spreadsheet or written list of problems to address. However, many developers have found that using a ready-made issue- or bug-tracking solution cuts time drastically. Its benefits include the ability to search issues, track their progress, document issues with notes and attachments, and assign issues to specific team members. Many digital developers make their issue tracker public so that their users can report bugs directly into the system. There are a number of free issue trackers available.

Another method for improving testing procedures is to use code validation. A variety of freely available tools can be used to review the programming code within an app or Web site and identify possible problems.

PRODUCT LAUNCH CHECKLIST

The following tasks need to be completed before your product's launch:

- Press release is written and ready to go out.
- Testing plan is in place. Full tests have been run, on hardware if applicable.
- Standards test has been completed, if applicable.
- Product has been submitted for approval, if applicable.
- User feedback and review system is in place and accessible.
- User support responsibilities are assigned.
- Product documentation and FAQs (frequently asked questions, with answers that will help users) are up-to-date.
- Launch has been announced on social networks and Web sites.

Organizations, such as the World Wide Web Consortium (W3C), are dedicated to furthering Web and application standards and often offer tools for reviewing Web page and code files for potential errors. By taking time to clean up and fix the issues identified, developers can hone their skills and avoid bigger problems down the road.

CHAPTER 6

CONTINUED DEVELOPMENT WITH UPDATES AND OPTIMIZATIONS

Creating valuable updates can be essential for maintaining a product and continuing its success well after the initial launch. The best approach for developing and deploying updates, whether you have a blog, Web site, mobile app, or game, is to have a well-thought-out strategy before making any changes. Updates are like product launches in miniature. In some ways they are riskier: they have the power to turn away existing users or attract new ones.

Your update plan should note how often an update will arrive and what primary features will be targeted. These can be wish list items that weren't ready for the initial release, top features requested by users, or adjustments to provide a better user experience. Each feature in the plan should include an estimate of the time and cost to implement it. This will help define the scope of each update. Be sure to balance the frequency of updates with the depth of features.

DESIGNING WITH METRICS

One of the most useful methods for guiding updates is to study the user metrics you have gathered. Incredibly valuable information can be garnered this way. For instance, seeing how many app downloads there are

GATHERING USER FEEDBACK

The following are useful tools for gathering feedback from users:

- IdeaScale allows users to submit feedback and vote for their biggest requests.

- Feedbackify allows users to respond to specific questions, as well as provide comments and ratings.

- Critique the Site allows Web developers to get feedback on a site's design.

- Usabilla allows for Web site usability testing with annotation and feedback.

- Bugzilla is a free issue-tracking software package that streamlines the job of prioritizing and documenting feedback requests, feature updates, and bug fixes.

per day can provide hints as to when the app is no longer drawing in new users. Web site logs often offer records of how many people visit the site each day, what hours they visit, which pages they view during the visit, and where they were coming from on the Web when visiting the site. This data can be used to identify pages on the site that are rarely visited. These logs also include errors or missing pages, which can help identify problems in the Web site code.

Using these metrics, you can find the right timing for an app update, breathing life into a product when the momentum from the initial launch begins to wane. If you have a Web site, you and your team can determine how often users return for new content and the best time to post new stories or blog entries. Identifying content that seems neglected by users may be a sign that the Web site's navigation menus are difficult to use.

There is a wide range of useful data sets that can be gathered from metrics and applied to updates. For instance, developer Snappy Touch added metrics to its iOS title Casey's Contraptions that would report approximately how long players took to complete each of the game's levels. The company could then use this information to adjust levels for difficulty ramping in future updates.

Learning to accept criticism will make reading reviews and feedback much more tolerable. Remember, every user has an opinion. Some of the most vital feedback can come from the users, and every change that addresses these items will be seen as hearing their pleas and catering to their needs. In fact, publicizing upcoming changes can help build interest and create word-of-mouth advertising for the product in a similar way as advertising before the initial launch.

Providing quick and direct methods for users to provide feedback can go a long way. Prompting a user to rate the app with an occasional pop-up, or allowing visitors to recommend a page directly to a search engine lets users add to the product's advertising with practically no cost to you. It also creates useful data that can be used when planning updates.

Consider the seriousness of each criticism when reviewing feedback. If a big problem is reported, something that hurts core features, it clearly becomes a big priority for the next update. If a small request is made by a number of users, your audience will appreciate your adding it. For the items that fit neither of these definitions, weigh the change's impact on the product against the time and cost to implement it. If you're working with a team, it can be useful to review these items as a group: getting several different views on a requested feature often yields a more elegant solution.

BUILDING ON SUCCESS WITH UPDATES

An update not only needs to introduce features that will attract new users, but it must also continue to please existing users. This makes the process of preparing users for an update an important one. Any big changes run the risk of confusing users, and confused users often go elsewhere out of frustration. Provide early instruction on new features and upgrades via tutorials and previews that highlight the benefits of the update. Products that update frequently, such as blog services with regular posts or the iOS Pocket God app, generate a user base that continues to visit to see

1 Seamless Messaging
2 Conversat History
Social box

Mark Zuckerberg, founder of Facebook, announces new updates to his social networking site in late 2010.

what the latest update has brought. The power of the update is a major factor in the success of today's digital products.

Testing for an update is just as important as testing for the initial release. It's best to test the full product, including all original content, not just the changed portions. Any change that's made could affect other areas unexpectedly. File size changes could create longer loading times on a Web site or memory problems on mobile platforms. In early 2011, an update to the

Facebook iOS app introduced a number of new features and fixes but, in the process, overlooked a bug that removed the ability to organize uploaded photos. The app's users reported the problem almost immediately, but it could easily have been avoided using a comprehensive test plan.

The process of launching an update is relatively similar to the initial launch. However, app update submissions typically see approval more quickly than the initial launch. Web updates are available the moment they're uploaded. The responsibility of watching for user response applies to updates as well: it will help the team develop the plan for the next update.

OPTIMIZING THE BUSINESS OF SUCCESS

Improving the process of development should always be at the top of a team's to-do list. One widely accepted method for this is the postmortem, a reflection on the process of developing a product. As its name hints, it's traditionally performed at the end of a project, but it can be just as successful at key development phases before the project is completed. The postmortem typically includes the top five or so successes, followed by the top five items that could be improved upon. It's possible to help direct future development by focusing on improving key areas of the team's process. Helpfully, many developers publish their postmortems online through trade Web zines, including Gamasutra, or on their own independent blogs.

If there is one last key to success when designing an update, it's the element of surprise. When a user discovers a hidden gem, it creates an attachment to the product that can lead to repeat use and word-of-mouth advertising. Providing that extra effort, even for something as small as a visual effect, encourages users to play with the product and feel that much more connected to it. A perfect example is the work Google puts into its search site logos and humorous search results.

The digital world presents today's entrepreneurs with exciting options never before available, including direct customer communication and the ability to make ongoing updates and improvements. Digital products have an eager market with a manageable learning curve for the self-starter. With proper planning and creativity, it's possible to build a unique digital product that becomes a real success.

GLOSSARY

ASP Active server page; a scripting language commonly used on Microsoft Web servers.

BLOG A frequently updated online journal, often expressing personal opinions.

BUG A software defect.

CONSUMABLE A purchase that is used immediately and can be repurchased at a later time.

CSS Cascading Style Sheets; a scripting language used to define visual formatting for Web site content.

FTP File Transfer Protocol; a commonly used method for sharing files over the Internet.

HTML HyperText Markup Language; a Web standard for displaying and formatting multimedia content on Web sites.

IN-APP PURCHASE A purchase made from within a mobile application.

JAVA The programming language most commonly used when developing Android apps.

METRICS Data gathered about a digital product and its users.

OBJECTIVE-C The programming language most commonly used when developing iOS apps.

PHP Hypertext Preprocessor; a scripting language commonly used for generating dynamic Web pages.

QA Quality assurance; the process of testing and verifying software for defects.

SDK Software development kit; a group of development tools and software used to create new software.

XML Extensible Markup Language; a customizable format for storing documentation commonly used on the Web.

American Society for Information Science and Technology (ASIS&T)

1320 Fenwick Lane, Suite 510
Silver Spring, MD 20910
(301) 495-0900
Web site: http://www.asis.org
The ASIS&T's mission is to advance the information sciences and related applications of information technology by providing focus, opportunity, and support to information professionals and organizations.

Association for Computing Machinery (ACM)

2 Penn Plaza, Suite 701
New York, NY 10121
(800) 342-6626
Web site: http://www.acm.org
The ACM is a membership organization for computing professionals working to advance computing as a science and a profession, to enable professional development, and to promote policies and research that benefit society.

Entertainment Software Rating Board (ESRB)

317 Madison Avenue, 22nd Floor
New York, NY 10017
Web site: http://www.esrb.org
The ESRB is a nonprofit body that assigns computer and video game content ratings, enforces industry-adopted advertising guidelines, and helps ensure responsible online privacy practices for the interactive entertainment software industry.

International Webmasters Association (IWA)
119 East Union Street, Suite #F
Pasadena, CA 91103
(626) 449-3709
Web site: http://www.iwanet.org
The IWA is the industry's recognized leader in providing educational and certification standards for Web professionals. It also offers specialized employment resources and technical assistance to individuals and businesses.

Media Awareness Network
1500 Merivale Road, 3rd Floor
Ottawa, ON K2E 6Z5
Canada
(613) 224-7721
Web site: http://www.media-awareness.ca
The Media Awareness Network creates media literacy programs for young people. The site contains educational games about the Internet and media.

WEB SITES

Due to the changing nature of Internet links, Rosen Publishing has developed an online list of Web sites related to the subject of this book. This site is updated regularly. Please use this link to access the list:

http://www.rosenlinks.com/deaa/goli

Allan, Alasdair. *Learning iPhone Programming*. Sebastopol, CA: O'Reilly, 2010.

Brathwaite, Brenda, and Ian Schreiber. *Challenges for Game Designers*. Boston, MA: Course Technology/ Cengage Learning, 2009.

Clark, Josh. *Tapworthy: Designing Great iPhone Apps*. Sebastopol, CA: O'Reilly, 2010.

Fenn, Donna. *Upstarts: How GenY Entrepreneurs Are Rocking the World of Business and 8 Ways You Can Profit from Their Success*. New York, NY: McGraw-Hill, 2010.

Fullerton, Tracy, Christopher Swain, and Steven Hoffman. *Game Design Workshop: A Playcentric Approach to Creating Innovative Games*. 2nd ed. Boston, MA: Elsevier Morgan Kaufmann, 2008.

Goldman, Jay. *Facebook Cookbook: Building Applications to Grow Your Facebook Empire*. Sebastopol, CA: O'Reilly, 2009.

Hoole, Gavin, and Cheryl Smith. *The Really, Really, Really Easy Step-by-Step Guide to Building Your Own Website for Absolute Beginners of All Ages*. London, England: New Holland, 2008.

Hussey, Tris. *Create Your Own Blog: 6 Easy Projects to Start Blogging Like a Pro*. Indianapolis, IN: Sams Publishing, 2010.

Hussey, Tris. *Using WordPress*. Indianapolis, IN: Que, 2011.

Jackson, Wallace. *Android Apps for Absolute Beginners*. Berkeley, CA: Apress, 2011.

Kerpen, Dave. *Likeable Social Media: How to Delight Your Customers, Create an Irresistible Brand, and Be

Generally Amazing on Facebook (and Other Social Networks). New York, NY: McGraw-Hill, 2011.

Kirkpatrick, David. *The Facebook Effect: The Inside Story of the Company That Is Connecting the World*. New York, NY: Simon & Schuster, 2010.

Lewis, Rory. *iPhone and iPad Apps for Absolute Beginners*. Berkeley, CA: Apress, 2010.

MacDonald, Matthew. *Creating a Website: The Missing Manual*. 3rd ed. Sebastopol, CA: O'Reilly, 2011.

Nixon, Robin. *Learning PHP, MySQL, and JavaScript*. Sebastopol, CA: O'Reilly, 2009.

Rowse, Darren, and Chris Garrett. *ProBlogger: Secrets for Blogging Your Way to a Six-Figure Income*. Hoboken, NJ: Wiley, 2010.

Schwartz, Brian. *50 Interviews: Entrepreneurs*. Denver, CO: Wise Media Group, 2009.

Selfridge, Benjamin, Peter Selfridge, and Jennifer Osburn. *A Teen's Guide to Creating Web Pages and Blogs*. Waco, TX: Prufrock Press, 2009.

Spinks-Burleson, Kimberly, and Robyn Collins. *Prepare to Be a Teen Millionaire*. Deerfield Beach, FL: Health Communications, 2008.

Wolber, David. *App Inventor: Create Your Own Android Apps*. Sebastopol, CA: O'Reilly, 2011.

BIBLIOGRAPHY

Dunlop, Michael. "Top Young Entrepreneurs Making Money Online." IncomeDiary.com. Retrieved September 24, 2011 (http://www.incomediary.com/top-young-entrepreneurs-making-money-online).

Gargenta, Marko. *Learning Android*. Sebastopol, CA: O'Reilly, 2011.

Hawker, Mark D. *The Developer's Guide to Social Programming: Building Social Context Using Facebook, Google Friend Connect, and the Twitter API*. Upper Saddle River, NJ: Addison Wesley, 2011.

Hockenberry, Craig. *iPhone App Development: The Missing Manual*. Sebastopol, CA: Pogue Press/O'Reilly, 2010.

ITProPortal.com. "Comparison of Various Software Development Life Cycle." July 4, 2010. Retrieved October 4, 2011 (http://www.itproportal.com/2010/07/04/comparison-various-software-development-life-cycle/?full).

Kim, Ryan. "One Third of Top-Grossing iPhone Apps Are Free." GigaOM.com, November 10, 2010. Retrieved September 24, 2011 (http://gigaom.com/2010/11/10/one-third-of-top-grossing-iphone-apps-are-free).

Learmonth, Michael. "Facebook 'Credits' Revenue Now Growing Faster Than Its Ads." AdAge.com, September 20, 2011. Retrieved September 24, 2011 (http://adage.com/article/digital/facebook-credits-revenue-growing-faster-ads/229874).

Lindahl, David, and Jonathan Rozek. *The Six-Figure Second Income: How to Start and Grow a Successful Online Business Without Quitting Your Day Job*. Hoboken, NJ: Wiley, 2010.

Mendez, Camella. "7 Critical Tips for Developing an iPhone App." *Internet Exposure*, August 19, 2011. Retrieved September 24, 2011 (http://www.iexposure.com/2011/08/19/critical-things-you-should-know-before-developing-an-iphone-app).

Plumley, George. *Website Design and Development: 100 Questions to Ask Before Building a Website*. Hoboken, NJ: Wiley, 2011.

Porter, Joshua. "The Freedom of Fast Iterations: How Netflix Designs a Winning Web Site." *User Interface Engineering*, November 14, 2006. Retrieved September 24, 2011 (http://www.uie.com/articles/fast_iterations).

Preston, Jennifer. "Social Media News Site Gains Clout." *New York Times*, October 2, 2011. Retrieved October 10, 2011 (http://www.nytimes.com/2011/10/03/business/media/mashable-once-a-one-man-blog-gains-clout-in-social-media.html?_r=1&scp=5&sq=digital%20entrepreneur&st=cse).

Romero, John. "Ravenwood Fair Post-Mortem." *Planet Romero*, 2011. Retrieved September 24, 2011 (http://planetromero.com/2011/03/ravenwood-fair-post-mortem).

Rowse, Darren. "13 Ways for Bloggers to Make Money with Advertising." Problogger.net, September 9, 2011. Retrieved September 24, 2011 (http://www.problogger.net/archives/2011/09/09/13-ways-for-bloggers-to-make-money-with-advertising).

Sande, Steven. "Report: In-App Purchases a Strong Source of iOS App Revenue." TUAW.com, September 22, 2011. Retrieved September 24, 2011 (http://www.tuaw.com/2011/09/22/report-in-app-purchases-a-strong-source-of-ios-app-revenue).

Schramm, Mike. "360iDev: How to Make Money from a Free App." TUAW.com, September 12, 2011. Retrieved October 4, 2011 (http://www.tuaw.com/2011/09/12/360idev-how-to-make-money-from-a-free-app).

Vercillo, Kathryn. "Young Entrepreneurs: Top 25 Teenage Millionaires." PromotionalCodes.org.uk, September 1, 2009. Retrieved September 24, 2011 (http://www.promotionalcodes.org.uk/6359/young-entrepreneurs-top-25-teenage-millionaires).

Yadav, Sid. "Facebook—The Complete Biography." Mashable.com, August 25, 2006. Retrieved September 24, 2011 (http://mashable.com/2006/08/25/facebook-profile).

Zimmerman, Eilene. "Teenagers Are Building Their Own Job Engine." *New York Times*, June 27, 2009. Retrieved September 24, 2011 (http://www.nytimes.com/2009/06/28/jobs/28teens.html).

Zimmerman, Eric. "Play as Research: The Iterative Design Process." July 8, 2003. Retrieved September 24, 2011 (http://www.ericzimmerman.com/texts/Iterative_Design.html).

INDEX

ABOUT THE AUTHOR

Colin Wilkinson is a professional video game developer and has previously operated a successful Web development company and nonprofit community arts organization and gallery. In between shipping games, he operates a small dairy farm with his wife in upstate New York.

PHOTO CREDITS

Cover, p. 1 (cityscape) © istockphoto.com/nadia; cover, p. 1 (hand, tablet) © istockphoto.com/artvea; pp. 3, 4–5 (numbers, laptops) © istockphoto.com/loops7; pp. 4 (inset image), 18, 21, 34, 38, 39, 42 © AP images; pp. 5 (bottom), 6, 14, 24, 35, 41, 48 © istockphoto.com/Dennis Glorie; pp. 7, 22 Bloomberg/Getty Images; p. 9 Hemera/Thinkstock; p. 12 Philippe Lopez/AFP/Getty Images; p. 15 © mackney/Alamy; p. 25 Paulsmith99/http://en.wikipedia.org/wiki/File:Waterfall_model_%281%29.svg; p. 52 Justin Sullivan/Getty Images; interior background image (glitter) © istockphoto.com/Tobias Helbig; remaining interior background image © istockphoto.com/Alexander Putyata.

Designer: Brian Garvey; Editor: Andrea Sclarow Paskoff; Photo Researcher: Amy Feinberg